*Praise Nothing*

# PRAISE NOTHING

*Poems by Joshua Robbins*

The University of Arkansas Press
*Fayetteville*
2013

ISBN-10: 1-55728-997-2
ISBN-13: 978-1-55728-997-1

17  16  15  14  13    5  4  3  2  1

*Designed by Liz Lester*


⊗ The paper used in this publication meets the minimum requirements
of the American National Standard for Permanence of Paper for
Printed Library Materials Z39.48-1984.


LIBRARY OF CONGRESS CATALOGING-IN-PUBLICATION DATA

Robbins, Joshua, 1979–
     [Poems. Selections]
     Praise nothing : poems / by Joshua Robbins.
          pages    cm
     ISBN-13: 978-1-55728-997-1 (paper : alk. paper)
     ISBN-10: 1-55728-997-2 (paper : alk. paper)
     I. Title.
     PS3618.O315235P73    2013
     811'.6—dc23
                              2012041670

# ACKNOWLEDGMENTS

Grateful acknowledgment is made to the editors of the publications where these poems first appeared, sometimes in slightly different form: *32 Poems* ("Praise Nothing"), *Apalachee Review* ("When I Say *Hymn*" and "Wash 'n' Shop"), *Briar Cliff Review* ("Dawn above Sacred Heart"), *The Canary* ("Yardscape Diagram, Good Friday"), *Carnelian* ("Equinoctial"), *Center* ("Doxology"), *Copper Nickel* ("A Force Too Familiar" and "A Patterning of Fire, a Gathering of Ash"), *DASH Literary Journal* ("Dithyramb with Streetlight"), *Fireweed: Poetry of Western Oregon* ("Washing in the Sangam"), *Fourteen Hills* ("Controlled Burn" and "Passing Paradise"), *Hayden's Ferry Review* ("Blue Spark"), *Linebreak* ("Heaven As Nothing but Distance"), *Mid-American Review* ("Against Forgiveness"), *New South* ("Field Rows" and "Field Guide to the Second Coming"), *Sonora Review* ("Sparrow" and "A Soul Petitions Entry"), *Southern Indiana Review* ("Of the Father"), *Southern Poetry Review* ("A Question of Ear"), *Still* ("Less Than Ash" and "Swing Low"), *Third Coast* ("Collateral"), *Tusculum Review* ("Attrition"), and *Waccamaw* ("Theodicy").

"Field Guide to the Second Coming" appeared in *Apocalypse Now: Poems and Prose from the End of Days*, edited by Andrew McFadyen-Ketchum and Alexander Lumans.

"Controlled Burn" appeared in *Best New Poets 2009*, edited by Kim Addonizio.

"Sparrow" appeared in *The Southern Poetry Anthology Volume VI: Tennessee*, edited by Jesse Graves, Paul Ruffin, and William Wright.

"Praise Nothing" appeared on the website *Verse Daily*.

"There Is a Fountain" appeared in *Writing By Ear: An Anthology of Writings About Music*, edited by Marianne Worthington.

Thanks to Larry Malley and everyone at the University of Arkansas Press. Thanks to Enid Shomer for her thoughtful readership and guidance.

Thanks to the institutions that provided me with support and employment during the years when these poems were written and revised:

the University of Oregon, Chemeketa Community College, and the University of Tennessee.

Thanks to Kim Addonizio, William Archila, Lory Bedikian, Marilyn Kallet, Laurie Lamon, T. R. Hummer, Larissa Szporluk, Pimone Triplett, Susan Wood, Robert Wrigley, Jake Adam York, and Paul Zimmer.

Many thanks to Dorianne Laux and Joseph Millar.

Many thanks to Garrett Hongo and Arthur Smith.

Special thanks to Jeffrey Schultz.

I could not have written these poems without the love, sacrifice, and patience of my wife, Emily. This book is for her.

# CONTENTS

### *A Patterning of Fire, a Gathering of Ash*

*Against Forgiveness*

## Against Forgiveness

In this life, nothing
        need be forgiven. Not
the streetlights' high murmur

        or the rattle of shopping carts
windblown across the parking lot.
        Not the skirr of asphalt

worn to gravel. What
        could be better? This slow
fade of sidewalk weeds

        and the sky's dingy light
spread like a rag over the faux-
        terracotta roof tiles

of the strip-mall liquor store,
        its sad neon wink,
its inventory of forgetting.

        Outside, a boy with spiked hair
and choke-chain collar waits
        for a buyer, and none of it

calls anything into question.
        So what is this need you have
to ask why you still

can't remember the name
of a lover you had once who could only
come in the backseat of your car,

who knew then that whatever
your thoughts of heaven
by now they'd be long

unutterable. Go ahead.
Take his money. No need
to remember. Buy him a fifth

of whatever's cheap. Pocket
the change and keep walking.

## Passing Paradise

Like a man blindfolded and asked to kneel
who cannot hear the bolt strike the cartridge
after it enters the chamber, its click
like classroom chalk breaking on black
slate, a sound small but definite:

                    one stone
kicked up against the curb, a pocketknife
shut, a finger snapped. So, what then
of the old Romanian sweeping the strip-mall
theater's sidewalk, for whom heaven
has become nothing

                but an age-dulled
marquee gone unlit for years,
its one *Paradiso* meant to entrance
whomever drives past and happens
to look up? I saw a film once in which
a wealthy man moved

                all he owned
into his parlor. Each morning, he fired
two rounds into the pile and, finding it
all still there, returned to sleep
beneath a thin blanket on the lacquered hardwood
of his indoor bowling lane.

                    It's not easy
to remember when we first began
to loathe irony. South of Bucharest and beside
the ditch banks and bare hills, the soaked

fields' sheen, where no one is asking if History
is yet up off its knees,

       powerful men
have reproduced TV's *Dallas* ranch. Weekend
getaways for sale. Even Larry Hagman's
been there. When he arrives, the executioner
carries the rifle indifferently,
swings it like a broom.

## Theodicy

Predestined for the warehouses
of the snow, cold sweeps east
across the asphalt, the darkening suburbs.

I think of Job and wonder
if God ever really returned
to business. After He'd consented

to boils and crushed livestock,
servants' and children's throats slit,
after ash, maybe one still afternoon

God raised both hands above His head
as if to say, "I've had enough,"
and renounced all of it,

took a job behind a desk
wearing khaki-colored scrubs,
filing papers to code and answering

the phones, His voice far away,
uninterested, yet familiar
to those desperate on the other end

of the line. If it were you
fidgeting in the waiting room,
you'd not even notice Him.

Just north past the ridgeline's barren
pin oaks, I watch in the rearview
as the office park's cold silhouette

dissolves into the outskirts
of suburban sprawl. If God is with us,
then maybe He lives around here, too,

some duplex on a loop or a single
apartment with a satellite dish. Maybe
right now God is, like us,

commuting across town toward home,
or headed from work to the store, or maybe
He's just driving, His window cracked

to feel the cold as the sun descends,
while the rest of us pull into our driveways,
jangle our keys at the front door, and try

to keep on believing, even as we
lock it behind us and turn out the light.

## Heaven As Nothing but Distance

Maybe it was enough to believe
    the zodiac's blazing entirety
would be cast from the sky,
    an effortless handful of salt

scattered to the Kansas plains'
    red wheat. Out West,
souls every day were shedding
    their earthly inheritance—the refused

histories of cause and effect,
    blight, hunger with a trace
of Santa Fe Railway coal
    dusting grocers' displays—

and so my grandfather, too,
    who, having left Topeka
for Los Angeles' early sprawl,
    exits the train station's dim

into day's white flash
    and takes one step onto his upturned
apple crate. A new Bible
    in his palm, he begins

to explain why all things are fire,
    what it is that makes you ache
awake. Once, on a gritty
    city beach in California, with flies,

stinking strands of rotting kelp,
        styrofoam, he and I sat watching
a gull choir first eyeball, then swoop,
        then peck, almost in unison,

something tangled in a blue tarp
        washed in above the tide's pull.
A drowning victim, maybe.
        A vagrant. And though we were

unable to see what was there,
        when he put his hand in mine
I could not even begin to count
        all the things I wished to believe in.

And that is how it would be
        if what I remembered was as true
as the waves landing, but now
        there is only the lungless

hot breath of L.A. on my cheek,
        the cries of gulls, their wings
ruffling into flight. The night after
        his memorial, someone

dug a hole into Kansas silt loam,
        dropped into it the plastic baggie
with his ashen remains. Nothing then
        but distance in every direction.

Above us, a satellite's beacon
        begged the horizon for home,
the heavens' scales measured the darkness,
        and that was all.

## Washing in the Sangam

The believers—villagers,
    astrologers, philanthropists,
        ash-smeared expatriates

and hippies seeking salvation—
    gather at the Sangam
        where the Yamuna's dark waters,

the brown currents of the Ganges,
    and the Saraswati converge.
        One man raises

his arms, wades
    chest high into polluted water.
        Another sings.

This one begs
    at the shoreline as dogs
        scavenge for food,

their long tongues lapping
    puddles of offered milk.
        Over our breakfast

of small handfuls of Cheerios,
    pieces of dry toast,
        five tangerine wedges,

I watch my son organize
        what I've provided: cold
                fruit centered down his

highchair's tray,
        the cereal and bread
                on either side.

Son, through faith
        you've found this hunger
                answered even as I

turn away in our ordinary house
        from the look of wonder
                in your face, the expression

Christ must have had
        seeing Lazarus raised,
                or the face of the Buddha

who looked behind him
        to find lotus blossoms
                opening in praise.

## Controlled Burn

after Hopper's *Office in Small City*


A kiss or rather the ruins of one: a swirl

of dust in sunlight, perhaps, as it mingles
    with the stifled love-cries of a hotel painting

above an unmade bed even after the lovers

    have left, checked out to wherever
lovers go hours later, driving a blue Chevrolet

    down a two-lane highway in Kansas

watching a controlled burn's flames
    flutter, smoke braids rising from black grass

to become the ashen haze of evening

    taking its regular inventory
of empty silos and sagging fence posts bound

    with rusted wire that mark the miles.

But whatever it is, I'll never know it, trapped
    as I am decades now, staring out spotless

window glass forever at God-knows-what.

    My sleeves rolled and vest chest tight,
this sun-muted office severe in its loneliness,

I know you're thinking I could be your father

years back, working late, distracted
        by the thought of a woman not your mother,

a woman who even now remains nameless,

        though it wasn't what you've thought: Motel 6
and an hour for lunch, Jim Beam in a plastic cup,

        lipstick-smeared menthols, the alarm buzzing

get back to work, as if in your imagining of it
        you might find some shadowed truth

made visible, something like what would find you here

        if you searched long enough, something there
in the foreground, maybe. Right there.

        Something knowable, touchable, a single stroke.

## Of the Father

Bolted down in the corner,
the black-and-white hospital set
rebroadcasts *Knute Rockne, All American*

and the Gipper's last wish. My father
stubs out another bummed smoke,
rolls his sleeves, exhales.

Through tear gas and batons,
he once linked arms with others
believing theirs would be the generation

to end it, but in this moment
he is thinking of the life he abandoned
in Kansas wearing down converts

with brimstone and ash, of his ghost-pained
brother who jumped from the roof
of the VA and died alone.

At the waiting room window,
he watches the afternoon drop
below Berkeley's hills, the traffic

up Ashby braking and coughing,
as down the hall his son
is born ten weeks too soon.

In a couple of months:
Inauguration Day, though already
school children are posed

as practice targets, their bodies
piled like cordwood in the streets,
their makeshift coffins scavenged

from the walls of bombed-out homes.
And somewhere the televised light
will remain the color of smoke

as twenty-one guns salute
and the world preps its cruelties.

## Less Than Ash

I'm beginning now to hear
the voice that sings just beyond memory:

heaven flung and not quite
an afterthought, something settling

on what shifts in the heart.
It's mid-summer now, and the sky

peels back above the turnpike
as another August late-afternoon

boils over. I remember the hard pew,
the voices singing, *Soon we'll reach*

*the shining river, soon our pilgrimage*
*will cease.* But here there is no ghost,

no elegy, and no wavering
*Amen* to be found in a hymn's last line

like the one I sang later, off key
and to no one in particular,

as I pulled the soiled mattress out
of the bedroom where my father died,

tipped it over the balcony railing
and onto the grass below.

Even then, what was it I wanted?
Not the river, its murmuring choir.

But something, yes. Something pure
like this asphalt steam's resurrection

of all I've forgotten or have tried
to forget: how after the service

behind the sanctuary, I wrote out
and diagramed my sins. How I'd lied.

Said I'd miss him. That I could hear him
singing with all of those called home.

Then, with no water to put it out
and wanting nothing more, nothing less

than ash, I held the paper, prayed
for a flame, struck the match.

## Equinoctial

Nearly October and the front oak's branches
    are mostly quicksilvered,

though we watch
    a handful here, a handful there

of leaves tinge copper.
    Beneath the zodiac's turning wheels

and the stars' nocturnal parade,
    the moon, pockmarked and mottled,

stamps night's scroll,
    and luminescent sealing wax

drips through leaf-lattice,
    puddles around our feet.

Caught in the celestial tilt-and-balance,
    we wear our brief freedom

like constellational moneychangers,
    all glitz and glimmer,

and weigh the disks of sun and moon
    like two coins on the pans of Libra's scales.

That is how it mostly goes.
    Blindly, we rummage around for an evener:

the black wick inside the candle's flame,
    our fingertips licked.

*Praise Nothing*

## *When I Say* Hymn

I mean breaker-crashed gunwales, yes,
     John Newton's near-shipwreck conversion,
and, of course, "Amazing Grace,"

     but as Janis Joplin screaked it,
her voice full throated and grainy
     bending the phrasing. And it's two

young men, homeless on a suburban
     church pew, one high or getting there,
the other striking matches,

     each small flame tossed
toward a pile of gasoline-soaked hymnals,
     and how the day after the fire

we sang over the sanctuary's
     ashy smolder. And it's the photo
tucked in my mother's Bible,

     the one she snapped circa 1967:
Pearl's mouth wailing, the stage
     set ablaze by the fiery coal

of her heart that Summer of Love.
     Sundays, having passed out
the night before, Mom would sing

*a wretch like me* tuneless
but extra loud, raise her Bible
    when the preacher's tongue

cast our sins away.
    How we burned then, bright
as when we first believed.

## Sparrow

A man doubles over
 to fit the angled crawl space

beneath the overpass,
 his makeshift shelter against January,

its icy transfiguration of every last
 façade and exposed city surface.

Surely he signifies something
 more than that which two

slumped shoulders and a sunken
 chest might represent to those

of us sleepless in surrounding
 subdivisions: the last unlit

match perhaps, which, when struck
 and held in the cup of a palm,

has everything to do with prayer.
 This much we know: no one thing

corresponds to any other.
 A midnight trucker's jake-braking

detonates sound-wall concrete,
 and we lie awake cursing

suburbia's toothless ordinances,
        which comforts no one and is useless

as questioning the possibility of mercy,
        that *His eye is on the sparrow.*

What I remember are weeknights
        spent at church, how the derelicts

gathered below on benches
        and cold pavement looked up

and how, first, we circled
        the upright, sang each verse

and refrain. Only then
        would we open our doors.

## There Is a Fountain

Gasoline stink of just-mowed dry grass,
    black-bagged trash, mulch,

station-wagon-oil driveway stains—out of these
    the melody of Midwestern drought:

this Sumac tremolo from a bird I can't name,
    this ash-gray lump trilling its fevered hymn

over the dusty tract-house roofs.
    Bird of Feathered Putty,

Bird of Oblivion's Blur, Smudge Bird,
    unlike you, I am exhausted

by the sky's indifference. The ground
    is cracked and the world

ready to blaze, yet I need nothing
    but this: your song filling

the cul-de-sac, your song of fire
    never burning out.

## Praise Nothing

April's cold snap
    fools next door's
lilac buds, glistens

    a white valediction
on last night's roadkill mange.
    And if this early

cardinal bloodying
    the fence line were
consolation to dawn's

    jerry-rigged claptrap
where cracked curb
    and razor gravel crosshatch,

I could listen
    to the trash can's
tipped-over plea, the skewbald

    *hallelu* of a dying lawn,
and praise nothing,
    let daybreak's

brokenness catch
    like glass shards in my throat
and not swallow.

# A Question of Ear

One by one, the street lamps' sodium purr clicks off
   as my neighbor's half-ton coughs
      and revs, coughs, and finally turns over

and he heads off, a gravel-tire churn
   as a gangsta rap bass line thumps from the cab,
      circles out like pond water

after a stone's plunk. "In the end it's all
   a question of ear," says Kierkegaard, meaning the *next* life:
      the next life as pure music, heaven's harmonic

resolve of Being's sour arpeggio. But for now,
   suburbia is tuned to dream's white noise,
      that octave three steps above wakefulness,

the one right before the clock radio
   bleeps on and the percolator autogrinds,
      and the front door rehearses its slam.

## Wash 'n' Shop

I'd like to say the scruffy anthem
a boy's rolled-up cuffs and scuffed sneakers
sing to a waning Saturday moon

and his midnight T.P.'ing of the neighborhood
are, together, a kind of code-breaking,
another tally slash in the column

*Unsuccessful Ciphers of the Outer World.*
But, as the Wash 'n' Shop's
double-stacked front loaders tumble and smack

in long rows, neither I nor his mother
getting high in the ladies' could care less
about the signified or how vent steam,

sweet smelling and inconsequential,
drifts upwards and becomes the sky.
So, tonight, let there be breakage.

Let the strip-mall bar next door empty out,
and let the half-tanked stumble home. Let not
one phrase of the turnpike's hum correspond.

## Dithyramb with Streetlight

There's a certain slant of dark, too,
        a streetlight's flicker, say, cast across
                a blocked-up Datsun's hood parked there

behind the vacant K-Mart where
        the kids get high to hoist themselves
                above the turnpike's high-pitched whine

in their blood, and they know there's no
        more to take from heaven, that all
                that's left is patched asphalt, chain-link.

## Swing Low

Easy to envy the juncos for their devotion to sky
and for how stupid they are, lured back down
to continue their frivolous songs
over rush hour's early stop-and-go.
                                    Surely nothing
is coming for to carry us home now.
This morning, more news of the same:
planes, body counts, incendiary clouds,
and a city burned alive as it slept.
                                    But what can I say of war?
The Midwestern clouds roll in with their sweaty air,
the sun rises rust tinged, and I go on
watching a few drab birds flit for seed in the spray
of sprinklers switching on.
                                    What consolation is there
to be found between heaven and earth,
between here and after? Nothing other
than the fading reassurance of stars
as day arrives slant
                        through darkened windows
the way, somewhere, a flourish of concertina wire
might urge us to believe that we'll all be written in,
be it the obits or *The Book of Life*,
and gathered then
                        like cloud shadows
over a street's parked cars and shop awnings
as we drag behind us the pale flags of our wings
and the birds cluster below and offer nothing
but the closed fists of their songs.

## Doxology

Because spring's grace by now
        is worth nothing more than the vacant wind
as it lays down cheat grass

        and smooth brome into the scrawled,
roadside shade of a hand-lettered
        billboard's *He is Risen,*

I can raise now this sweating
        and half-empty longneck
to August's full bloom and bring it

        back to the lips half full,
blessed by whatever it is
        that jinks the last monarchs

fluttering like quarter notes over the driveway,
        its flat, sun-glittered tongue,
its hymn of sawdusted motor oil

        ascending into nothing
but the wash line's pinned-up T-shirts
        and damp shorts flapping pointless

as prayer flags in the sweltering breeze.
        And although fall's back soon
with its hard tally of leaf change

and leaf drop, its apostate
yawn of jaundiced light
        hung in the barren trees

like torn sackcloth, I'm content
        for now to love, to watch
summer's penitents stumble

        down the path of sweat and sacrifice:
contrite women with bad knees
        and sensible shoes, young mothers

like exhausted pilgrims
        pushing their chubby toddlers
who point to the empty sky,

        even the bare-chested young men
who jog the tortured asphalt
        with furrowed brows seared

by August's mark and headed
        God-knows-where, who know
we all take nothing with us,

        not even the relief of these
our long purgatorial shadows.

## Field Rows

Crossed-out and re-circled,
the *Want Ads'* daily litany
of numbers and names lies crumpled
on the bar where loose change

for the busted jukebox stacks up,
mini nickel-plated silos
looming lusterless over dusty
mahogany laminate plains.

Not that there's much chance
this out-of-work road crew
in born-again Kansas would ever
be seen toe-tapping to any

pentatonic lick, let alone
a proper blues, now that crude
is surging again and the county seat
has slashed dollars for paving.

Even ten years back:
Kaw River corn, grain sorghum,
soybeans. Now, new fields
sit fallow: stray strip-mall

girders, an LED billboard
scrolling *The Future Home of* . . .
and *Brought to You by* . . . as heat
coronas skyward from base layer hot mix

like burnt offering stink rising
to the small gods of sprawl
whose red ink outstrips
and dries up work.

And yet, in the rusty light
from the TV, the bar's
empty tallboys glint as if
they still had pull, as if we

might become something more
than divine backwash, something other
than broke, even the one of us
in the back booth lounging

on yellow Naugahyde and trying
to foretell the aftermath of agribusiness
subsidies and a dwindling tax base,
though surely no bottle's

peeled-back label will ever
reveal anything other than darkened
glass. Besides, what is
the chapter and verse of who

owes what? In a couple of hours,
this place will clear. Someone
will sign a slip for the tab
or else skip out. Someone's truck

will roll into the ditch and he'll walk
field rows back toward town.
And someone heading north
will tune in "The Gospel Highway"

and drive until the signal fades,
until smoke blooms
from the tailpipe, white
as the damning lilies of the field.

*Collateral*

## Collateral

Once I watched my neighbor, returned
         from the gulf, bring a weathered length

of scrap two-by-four down, without
         hesitating, upon the wrecked

spine of a Dalmatian stray. Weeks
         he'd kept her in the alleyway

behind the garage, her neck tied
         to his Ford with an extension

cord. Nights, after he'd stumble home
         drunk, I'd listen to him shout and

lay into her until he was
         done. In that moment though, it was

as if this world had never been
         more pure, that the rasped October

breeze through the birch trees on our street
         meant nothing, saw nothing, could say

nothing. There was only silence,
         then a clang of wood on concrete

and, somewhere, the dead leaves stirring.

### A Soul Petitions Entry

"Big Bopper's casket destined for eBay"
—AP headline, 12/31/08

Let heaven be not a long ways off
     from our crash into field rows outside Clear Lake, Iowa, Lord,

and let my soul be equally as trifling in your sight
     as Holly's Beechcraft Bonanza,

though may my flight to your right side
     take the exact reverse trajectory.

And please bless Waylon Jennings,
     who knew not what he did, Lord,

and couldn't know that when they did bury me
     it'd be with my hair coiffed and socks but no shoes

in 16-gauge Batesville Casket steel,
     which now must be prepped and re-shined for digital sale,

though it suffers from only minor rust and a few white lime stains
     after years in Beaumont clay.

Let my trespasses be equally scrubbed in your sight, Lord.
     Bestow on me today your grace

like *whshhhoooh White Lightning,*
     and may my reward be to glimmer

like a Wurlitzer bubble in color-changing neon, Lord,
     even as this song ends and the next begins.

## A Force Too Familiar

As if discipline might choke back
    the syncopate chime of the church bells'

round tones and what I could not yet
    distinguish as want, I sat waiting

on the church front's wide steps, an Ash Wednesday
    soot cross smudged

on my forehead, and counted
    the passing cars caught

in plate glass reflections. Beneath
    the sky's after-services light, everything

had the consciousness of the angelic:
    opalescent wings of pigeons preening

in the shadows of the open double doors.
    The rumpled slacks of young men

pushing their way out. The glint of windshields
    and chrome, and then the groan

of my friend's car pulling up
    to the gutter. Even his hand,

the shape of its motioning. Even
    his hand, golden in that light,

became the hand that holds
　　the shining keys of what was

and is to come, and what did
　　was this: spilled Bud on the back seat,

a five-dollar bill pressed
　　into my sweaty palm, then a fumbling

of button fly and his tongue
　　a close rhyme of desire and cold sky.

Above us, the spring stars were a force
　　too familiar to recognize, as if the harmonies

of life and life were the most
　　transparent thing in this world, as if being

meant more than to shudder
　　beneath their glare.

## Blue Spark

Back deck, Adirondack: evening hums.
    Fly-by-nights kamikaze iridescence
into the zapper's electric blue.

    Due west and past the river,
thunderclouds horizon summer's
    thirsty ridgeline, and I, moth

to fluorescence, stalk the moon.
    Once, in a bar's back booth,
I was flesh jolted AC.

    In the dance floor's strobe,
I radiated Plato, the Whitmanesque,
    flashed the poetry of drag

and chrome, glittered vinyl, tiger print.
    Outside, the city's turbines
churned the river's darkness white.

    Now, summer rain
on oil-stained driveways, backed-up gutters,
    the low river's drift.

Lightning spikes. I inhale the night:
    lawn mist. Insect char. Beyond
the clouds, the electric moon.

## Dawn above Sacred Heart

Too easy to remember April and call it
*cruel*: the precise sutures of crows

across the wires, the low rooftops' tar
oily and frost scabbed under brown fog

as the hospital-gowned light of false dawn
thinned over the commuter's stop-and-go

and the river's broken prosody.
No sleep. All night a manic *De profundis*,

its metrics a static fused to the drug-bisected
prayers offered by any one of us there:

Sacred Heart, its upper chamber
aflame nightly with the amalgamated light

of ward fluorescence and the psychotics' hellfire,
the flicker behind the eyes of the woman

who reopened her arm. And I would like
to believe what was released then by broken

glass is describable now in the language
of the living, but years later, she is still

on her knees wailing her ruptured prayer
as the city below bleeds out into day.

## Attrition

Stranded along the interstate
    and hoping the red blinking
        might be a far-off sheriff's

cruiser and not the sleepy
    Morse of hazard bulbs
        on empty grain silos,

their spent concrete stave
    shadows braced hard
        against the tired lean

of wrack-framed barns,
    I sift the radio's slow
        fade: '70s AM

starlet belting something
    like, "It's no use,"
        the signal sputtering

further into white noise
    with each tractor-trailer
        grinding by.

Across acres of flat,
    the Kansas dusk drops
        its dusty partition

of crop chemicals, exhaust
        from pickups headed home,
                and I stare out the grimed windshield

watching a black scrim
        of starlings scatter,
                re-collect over

the highway's ditch. Again
        and again they lift up,
                a fist in the dry wind,

and return broken
        to the prairie's dull ache.
                When darkness falls, they'll fly

off for the horizon, the edge
        of a distant field, settle there
                among the dirt, the chaff.

## Field Guide to the Second Coming

It will be sudden and flash
like bottle shards or like morning
fracturing against the horizon's
edge of strip-mall rooftops
and be a comfort and turn a few
bucks into fistfuls of ordinary
joy expanding in the capillaries
of whoever no longer desires
to sleep there between buildings
as traffic picks up beneath
the telephone wires' high operatics
and it will sing, of course, and be
sung by the gravel-throated
*hallelujahs* of dumpsters raised up
and emptied into the truck's dark
which could be something like
a metaphor for grace though nothing
is new here under the sun
beating down in mid-April
where no one is looking for the infinite
and the endlessness one imagines
must come after death
seems like nothing more
than a voice in the void, a strike
of the heel, an empty tomb.

## Yardscape Diagram, Good Friday

Late-March, postlapsarian afternoon.
      In this season, metaphysical veins get tapped.

Sometimes like flesh-digging with a needle, uneasily.
      Sometimes like a single hammer blow, the nail

driven all the way through: illumination exploding
      into the world like the trumpeted heads of fuchsia,

the crocuses' purple song, paradise-edge
      of agapanthus and bacopa. It took weeks

to wrench-up and haul away the planking
      and joists from the worn-out redwood deck,

only a Friday to pour the porch's quick-dry
      cement slab. Like a side-fallen tombstone it waits

for the decorative ordination of potted flora
      I'll place just so, each clay pot

filled with a measure of earth, a measure of devotion.
      Clock-tick approaching the afternoon's fourth hour.

Diminished probability the sun will fully prick through
      the clouds, the sky's thin arteries that streak-erase

a dusk-at-hand blue to blank white.
      In light such as this, any upward progress

I've made seems otherwise, and the harsh incline
    of worldly purgation stretched-out beyond

my stride like an absolute. But even so,
    life journeys forward, composes its metaphors.

Sometimes of language transparent as flesh.
    Sometimes of language that settles like dust

slant into late-afternoon. Sometimes of light
    set off in the pear tree's white bloom,

piercing the gray matter, rushing into the soul.

*A Patterning of Fire, a Gathering of Ash*

## A Patterning of Fire, a Gathering of Ash

In the anatomy classroom,
    the clock's red second hand
        is nothing if not devoted

to itself, its protracted
    humming revolution low
        like a sonic monument

to boredom or a spell
    conjured by Time
        and cast over rows

of students sleepy and sated
    on afternoon heat, the pollen's
        Brownian motion.

I remember the plastic
    models of the body:
        human head

split down the middle,
    heart's anterior view,
        cartoon-like cutaways

of lungs, paired carotids.
    Never did we connect
        our own young bodies' end

to Zippo thumbwheel, naphtha
    flame, the gravity bong.
        And why would we?

Each afternoon senior year,
　　　my girlfriend and I
　　　　　would hotbox her father's

junk-cramped singlewide,
　　　exhale our respective plans
　　　　　for work or moving out

and her wish to finally
　　　be rid of him. In the end,
　　　　　we'd little of all of it,

which is to say, in the end,
　　　all of it burned.
　　　　　Before she left, moved north,

we took up nights
　　　in a department store's stockroom
　　　　　unloading freight,

crates resembling the kind
　　　from early-Saturday TV,
　　　　　those ones marked *HANDLE WITH CARE*

and *DANGER*, and always that sympathetic
　　　villain surrounded by TNT,
　　　　　then the long fuse lit,

then a look of quiet
　　　acquiescence as the blue
　　　　　sparks flared toward detonation.

She was an addict by then
　　　and hired to wipe dust
　　　　　off cheap trinkets, bookshelf

knickknacks, the tiny blown glass
        figurines I pulled from Styrofoam
                and packing straw. "Can you

believe this shit?"
        Her single question repeated
                again and again under the HVAC's

metallic drone, her words
        signifying less each time
                she glanced up from her table

and damp rag, her eyes
        bloodshot as if an explosive
                occlusion, some errant

syringe push's bubble
        of air deep in a vein's
                claustrophobic dark,

were rigged, gone haywire,
        a conflagration set off
                in her blood, which is

one way out, perhaps.
        Which was hers.
                In her face the day she left,

Time lay open.
        Pure; skeletal.
                We believed in nothing then,

which hardly had to do
        with us because already
                the tired, blind hands

of statistics—addictions
   and foreclosures, all the anonymous
      desperations of the elect—

had blessed us, pressed
   their cindered palms against
      our foreheads, and we

understood all of it,
   how every thing submits
      in the end

to the elemental will
   of ash. Three days ago,
      a high school girl vanished,

and because she was no runaway
   and because there'll be
      no dumpstered duffle

found days later
   jam packed with spare clothes,
      butane refills, Pyrex tubes

stolen from the school's
   chem lab racks, and so
      none of inevitability's

backstreet Meth mouth,
   scabs, it becomes easier
      to question how it is

a body becomes nothing,
   because we know it's only
      a matter of time before the patrol car's

swiveling searchlight coerces
warehouse shadows to confess
the bodies of the beaten

or worse. Then,
bag and tag and two
licked fingers riffling

a ledger's stained columns,
a greasy index dialing
the next of kin,

like Thomas who placed his finger
into the resurrected void
of Christ's side, which was

both there and gone,
who knew then that whether
on earth or as it is

in heaven, living meant
going on without
all that'd been left behind.

The blast, officials said,
resulted from a fireplace gas leak
negligible enough to have gone

unnoticed—a slow-moving cloud
over the developing cul-de-sac,
a mansion in the sky—

until a single match strike,
as in the slow motion of dream,
shot an instant of light,

then heat, then fire,
from basement subfloor
and out into the unfinished

subdivision's million-dollar frames,
and lifted her parents from sleep
and from sleep's second story

interrogation of their underwater mortgage,
how, maybe, it'd be best
to just drop the keys

into the branch manager's
cupped hands and walk away.
Later, someone found

my girlfriend's body,
her small frame collapsed
on itself between snow drifts.

Not long after hearing this,
her father, drunk,
stubbed out a smoke

on the trailer's blue shag.
Even hours after the fire,
after neighbor men had dug in

and scattered suppressing sand,
shovelfuls of gravel
over the grassless hard clay,

the charred ground still
sent up curls of white
chemical smoke

that kissed their bare ankles
          as if its touch were final,
                    as if the future were known.

What do you do when shame
          and that which seems like chance
                    combine, so that if you

and therefore I, or, if anyone,
          had stood there fixed,
                    shoeless, naked to the waist

beside them, we would each
          be revealed as nothing
                    ourselves and worthless

before the flames,
          because if it is true
                    that one must descend

because it is one of the styles
          of hell, and if it is meant
                    to take a while,

then it isn't the fire's
          withered hands peeling back
                    the roof's blistered shingles,

nor the way heat's rage
          makes of the contracting space
                    between drywall a smoldering

lung, warping sheet aluminum,
          splitting joists and trusses,
                    and finally cleaving

the trailer's prefab entirety,
    the whole damn thing
        fallen in on itself,

that makes it impossible
    to find your own face
        in the flames. It is the ash.

The ash that fills the air
    and blinds us as we
        go down unguided,

together, and must do so
    until we have arrived, reconciled,
        to go on living there

below with all we have
    forgotten, to go on living
        there with everything.

# NOTES

### Passing Paradise

A resort in Slobozia, Romania, boasts a near-replica of the ranch from the American primetime soap opera *Dallas*. The actor Larry Hagman played the main character J. R. Ewing for the series's entire run. The film referenced is Paul Thomas Anderson's *There Will Be Blood*.

### Theodicy

Job 38:22–23: "Have you entered the warehouses of the snow or seen the storehouses of the hail, which I reserve for times of trouble, for days of war and battle?"

### Washing in the Sangam

The Triveni Sangam is the location where the Yamuna and Ganges Rivers meet the mythological Saraswati River near Allahabad, India. It is the site of Kumbh Mela, a massive Hindu pilgrimage that concludes with ritualistic bathing on the banks of these waters.

### Controlled Burn

The poem responds to Edward Hopper's 1953 painting *Office in a Small City*.

### Of the Father

The 1940 film *Knute Rockne, All American* starred Ronald Reagan as George "The Gipper" Gipp.

### Less Than Ash

The quote is from the hymn "Shall We Gather at the River?" written by Robert Lowry in 1864.

### *When I Say* Hymn

The hymn "Amazing Grace" was written in 1748 by English poet, clergyman, and abolitionist John Newton. Janis Joplin, nicknamed "Pearl," performed the hymn in San Francisco, January 31, 1967.

### *Sparrow*

The quote is from the hymn "His Eye Is on the Sparrow" written by Civilla D. Martin in 1905.

### *There Is a Fountain*

The poem responds to the hymn by the same title written by English clergyman and poet William Cowper in 1772.

### *A Question of Ear*

The quote is from Søren Kierkegaard's *Papers and Journals: A Selection* (Penguin, 1996).

### *Swing Low*

The poem alludes to the hymn "Swing Low, Sweet Chariot" written by Wallis Willis in 1862.

### *Doxology*

The specific doxology the poem responds to is "Praise God, from Whom All Blessings Flow," written by Thomas Ken in 1674. It is perhaps the most widely sung hymn in the world.

### *A Soul Petitions Entry*

J. P. "The Big Bopper" Richardson died with Buddy Holly and Ritchie Valens when Holly's plane crashed February 3, 1959. Waylon Jennings gave up his seat on the plane to Richardson, who had a cold. The famous George Jones song "White Lightning" was written by The Big Bopper. In 2007, The Big Bopper's son, Jay, exhumed his father's coffin and in 2008 announced he would sell the coffin on eBay.